FRIENDS
OF ACPL

D1246669

The harp that once through Tara's halls
its soul of music shed,
Now hangs as mute on Tara's walls
as if that soul were fled.

Ireland

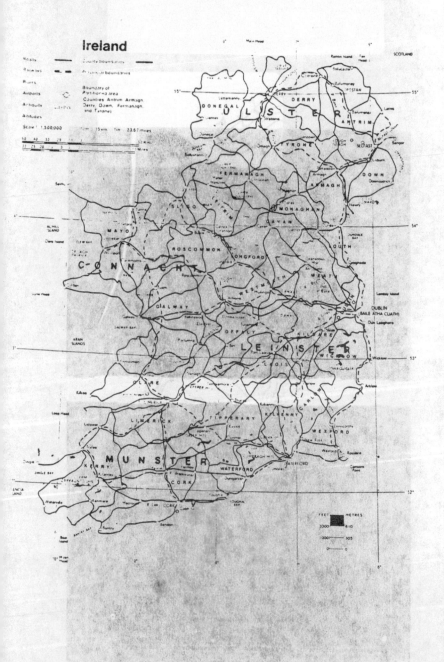

IRISH

COUNTRY COOKING

by

Norma and Gordon Latimer

Compiled and published by:
Norma and Gordon Latimer
2639 S. Van Buren Pl. Los Angeles, CA. 90007
Drawings by Jan Dungan

ISBN 0-941869-03-2

TABLE OF CONTENTS

Page

Apple Barley Flummery............56
Apple Brack......................50
Bacon Broth......................16
Barm Brach.......................52
Beef Broth.......................16
Beef Olives......................43
Bishop's Night Cap...............73
Black Cap Pudding................76
Black Pudding....................38
Blancmange.......................74
Boiled Cake......................49
Boxty Bread......................22
Braised Goose....................33
Brandy Sauce.....................58
Burnt Oranges....................51
Burnt Sugar Sauce................57
Buttermilk Bread.................25
Cally, Poundies, Pandy...........21
Carrageen Cream or Syrup.........78
Carrot Soup......................13
Celery Soup......................14
Champ or Stelk...................21
Clear Soup.......................12
Cockle Soup.......................3
Cod with Cockles.................45
Colcannon........................44
Convent Eggs.....................27
Corned Beef and Cabbage..........28
Creamed Cabbage..................32
Crubins Pea Soup.................10
Donegal Pies.....................30
Dublin Bay Prawns................23
Dublin Coddle....................39
Dublin Rock......................61
Dumplings........................15

TABLE OF CONTENTS

Page

Egg Cutlets...........................17
Fadge.................................47
Flaky Pastry..........................80
Guinness Cake.........................55
Guinness Christmas Pudding............59
Gur Cake..............................64
Hot Water Pastry......................80
Irish Coffee..........................79
Irish Hunter's Pie....................36
Irish Mist Cream......................77
Irish Stew............................24
Irish Treacle Loaf....................50
Irish Whiskey Butter..................60
Irish Whiskey Cake....................69
Leek and Oatmeal Soup..................6
Mead..................................72
Michael Kelley's Sauce................41
Mussel Soup............................4
Mutton Broth..........................16
Mutton Pies...........................37
Nettle Soup............................8
Oatcakes..............................53
Oatmeal Pastry........................82
Onion Soup............................11
Pea Soup...............................9
Pig's Trotters Crubeens...............40
Pork Ciste............................31
Porridge..............................63
Porter Cake...........................67
Porter Pudding........................58
Potato and Apple Cake.................62
Potato Pastry.........................82
Potato Scones.........................49
Potato Soup............................1
Potted Crab...........................46

TABLE OF CONTENTS

Page

Rough Puff Pastry....................84
Scailtin.............................73
Scallops with Mushrooms.............26
Scones..............................48
Seed Cake...........................66
Shortbread..........................70
Short Crust Pastry..................83
Soda Bread..........................25
Spatchcock..........................42
Spiced Beef.........................18
Steak with Whiskey..................34
Suet Pastry.........................82
Syllabub............................75
Traditional Pate....................19
Tipsy Cake..........................68
Tripe and Onions....................29
Turnip Soup..........................5
Urney Pudding.......................71
Watercress Soup......................7
Water Biscuits......................35
Wicklow Pancake.....................19
Yellowman...........................65

HERBS AND SPICES

Keep a good selection of spices and herbs in your store cupboard, for a well-flavoured dish is more interesting and it can tempt even a jaded palate, as it acts upon the taste buds and stimulates the gastric juices. Spices are obtainable in various forms, the most convenient being powdered--sold in drums--which keep almost indefinitely in a cool, dry place. Many herbs may be grown in a garden or window box. When fresh herbs are unobtainable, use dried herbs--either those you have prepared yourself or purchased in drums or packets.

TO DRY HERBS

Wash then after picking in hot weather, dry well in a cloth, then lay them on baking trays, padded with plenty of paper and a piece of muslin over the top. Dry very slowly in the airing cupboard or very low oven (with the door ajar) until brittle. Crumble then store in airtight tins or jars. In very hot weather they can be dried in the sun. Tie in bundles and protect from flies and dust by putting muslin over them. Parsley is a better colour if dried for a few minutes in a hot oven.

WEIGHTS AND MEASURES

Throughout this book, American weights and measures have been used.
For interest and for reference, differences between Irish and American measures have been included.

SOLID MEASURES IRISH (AND USED IN CANADA)	AMERICAN (AND IN AUSTRALIA)
1 lb. butter or other fat............2 cups
1 lb. flour.........................4 cups**
1 lb. granulated or castor sugar.....2 cups
1 lb. icing or confectioner's sugar..3 cups
1 lb. brown sugar...................2½ cups
1 lb. golden syrup or treacle........1 cup
1 lb. rice.........................2 cups
1 lb. dried fruit...................2 cups
1 lb. chopped meat..................2 cups
1 lb. lentils or split peas.........2 cups
1 lb. coffee (unground)..............2½ cups
1 lb. soft breadcrumbs ....4 cups
½ oz. flour....................1 level tablsp.*
1 oz. flour....................1 heaped tablsp.
1 oz. sugar....................1 level tablsp.
½ oz. butter...................1 level tablsp.
1 oz. golden syrup or treacle..1 level tablsp.
1 oz. jam or jelly.............1 level tablsp.

* must be standard measuring tablespoon
** ALL RECIPES USE SELF RAISING FLOUR UNLESS OTHERWISE INDICATED

LIQUID MEASURES

The most important difference to be noted is that the American pint is 16 fluid ounces as opposed to the Irish pint, which is 20 fluid ounces. The American ½-pint measuring cup, therefore, is actually equivalent to two-fifths of an Irish pint. While Canadian housewives use many American recipes and American measures, they are used to calculating in terms of the 20 ounce pint. In Australia 1-pint is 20 liquid ounces, but when measuring solid ingredients an 8-ounce cup measure is used.

SEE AT A GLANCE........

1½ pints......3-3/4	American cups
1 pint.......2½	American cups
½ pint.......1¼	American cups
¼ pint.......5/8	American cups

A SHORT HISTORY OF IRELAND

Irish history begins with the invasion of the Gaels in the first century B.C., a branch of the Celts who swept Europe centuries before the Christian era, who brought the ancient Irish language and culture with them. Monks developed a written Irish language and transcribed Gaelic lore and tradition. Pagan and Christian decorative art merged in exquisite illuminated manuscripts, such as the Book of Kells.

The Vikings throughout the ninth and tenth centuries plundered the monasteries. Political change altered Gaelic culture, when small kingdoms were consolidated into realms that remain today as Ireland's four provinces: Munster, Connaught, Leinster and Ulster. Anglo-Norman England entered Ireland in the 12th Century and by 1250 the Normans had gained control over three-quarters of Ireland. Gradually the Normans merged with the Gaelic families and the Anglo-Normans became Gaelo-Normans, intermarrying and adopting Irish ways.

By 1400 the area known as the Pale (where English law was observed and enforced) extended only slightly beyond Dublin--where the term "beyond the pale" originated. The Irish were not only attacked by the English but also the Spanish. By 1640 the Protestant Scots and English had formed a majority of landowners in Ulster. A mid-17th Century island rebellion was quelled by Oliver Cromwell and by the century's end Protestants, being 20% of the population, owned 86% of Ireland.

The Anglo-Irish prospered during the 1700s and in 1801 the Act of Union joined Ireland to the United Kingdom. Repeated efforts were made to repeal the Act without success and then came the potato famine, 1845-51, causing many to emigrate to the United States, resulting in a great decline in the population. Still much turmoil prevailed and in 1922 there was a truce which divided Ireland into the Irish Free State and Northern Ireland. The Irish Free State withdrew from the Commonwealth in 1949 to become the completely independent Republic of Ireland, called Eire in Gaelic.

The national flag is a tricolour of green, white and orange arranged vertically with the green nearest the flagstaff. Green represents the older Gaelic and Norman-Irish element in the population, orange for the supporters of William of Orange in the wars at the end of the 17th Century. The flag was first adopted in 1848 by members of the Young Ireland movement. The white in the centre signifies a lasting truce between the "Orange" and the "Green."

The Irish Constitution provides that Irish, as the national language, shall be the first official language of Ireland. It recognizes the English language as a second official language. Irish belongs to the Guidelic branch of Celtic, one of the four original languages of Western Europe, and is also the oldest written vernacular in Europe, after Greek and Latin. It is basically the same as the Gaelic of Scotland and is related to Welsh, Breton and ancient Gaulish.

GAELIC LANGUAGES

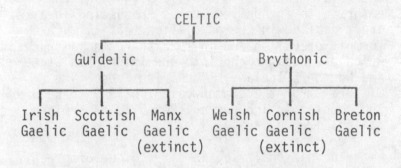

CELTIC

Guidelic — Brythonic

Irish Gaelic — Scottish Gaelic — Manx Gaelic (extinct) — Welsh Gaelic — Cornish Gaelic (extinct) — Breton Gaelic

"THE EMERALD ISLE"

Ireland is a small island of approximately 32,000 square miles, with gentle rolling plains and heavily forested highlands, beautiful lakes and swampy bogs, with rocky cliffs leading to the stormy Irish Sea on the east coast and the far reaching Atlantic on the west coast.

Ireland is a well-known haven for writers because of an ancient law excluding them from paying income tax. Among its great writers are Oscar Wilde, George Bernard Shaw, James Joyce, to mention but a few.

Ireland is not only the land of the potato but also of good tasting lamb, beef, marvelous Limerick hams, and bountiful streams of salmon, and a coastline filled with oysters, lobster and mussels.

Ireland has high quality crafts such as Waterford hand-blown crystal, traditional Aran sweaters and tweeds woven in several areas, the most notable being Donegal. There is also the lovely hand-embroidered Irish linen, and the delicate Belleek China.

For centuries the Irish have played their lively music on instruments like the uilleann (elbow) pipes, the fiddle and flute, and have entertained themselves with their traditional Irish dancing.

> *"Ireland is like no other place under heaven, and no man can touch its sod or breathe its air without becoming better or worse."*

George Bernard Shaw

MYTHOLOGY OF IRELAND

Mythologies tend to be originally based on fact, and gradually modified through time. The early history of Ireland is one such case. As the early Celtic culture was a verbal one, not written, the history was recorded as an oral tradition.

Mythology records that five successive groups of invaders occupied Ireland before the early Celts eventually settled there. The first invader was a woman called Cessair and her female expedition. They all perished in the Great Flood. Several hundred years later the Partholon arrived; they eventually died in the Great Plague. Nemed came next. Although he died, his people lived on and eventually abandoned the country and split into three groups. The first group was called the Fir Bolg, who remained in Ireland. The second were Nemeds company and the third were the last group of invaders of Ireland, the Tuatha De Danann. The Tuatha De Danann (people of the Goddess Danann) fought the Fir Bolg in the first battle of Mag Tuired for control of Ireland. The battle ended in a pact of peace, goodwill and friendship. Later, another group, the Fomorians, tried to invade Ireland. They were of humanoid shape but had only one large leg and one large arm and eyes in their back. The Tuatha De Danann managed to repel the Fomorians in the second battle of Mag Tuired. Before the Fomorians had come to Ireland, there had been a marriage between the Fomorian king and the Tuatha queen. From this union was born Lug, a very powerful person, and a hero in Celtic mythology.

Another great hero of Celtic mythology is Cuchulainn. His father was Sualdam and his mother was King Conchobor's sister. When he

was born he was called Setanta and excelled in
many sports. He acquired the name Cuchulainn
(meaning Hound of Culann) by fighting Culanns
savage dog, and killing him. More mythology
of Cuchulainn can be found in Tain bo Cuailnge.

Mythology played a large part in Celtic
culture, as the history and tradition was
passed on from generation to generation in
these long tales. The Tain bo Cuailnge is
one of the earliest pieces of Celtic litera-
ture, dating from the 8th Century. It is
commonly taught in Ireland as a 'fairy' story
as mythology is still very much alive in
Ireland.

IRISH WHISKEY

The word 'whiskey' comes originally from Irish uisce beatha, literally 'the water of life.' The word has re-entered the language in some areas as fuisce (fwishka), more common in Connacht than elsewhere, and uisce beatha is still the more common form of the word. Poitin (potcheen) is the word for home-made whiskey. Poitin is made in almost all parts of Ireland, but it has a particularly strong association with Gaeltacht areas. (Districts in which Irish is still spoken habitually are known as 'An Ghaeltacht' and these are mainly situated on the west coast; Donegal where 'Ulster Irish' is spoken, Galway and north Mayo where 'Connacht Irish' is spoken, and parts of Cork, Kerry and Waterford where 'Munster Irish' is the usual dialect.

Poitin is made from potatoes but also from numerous vegetable products, but always a traditional recipe. It has a certain rough- ness to its taste, especially to the un- accustomed drinker. Poitin must be taken with caution as its effects can be devastating.

In any case, making it is an offence, with severe penalties.

THE FLAVOUR OF IRELAND

Irish cooking is probably looked upon as a farmhouse cuisine with much of the food being grown on small farms for their own personal needs, rather than an international cuisine. Many Irish traditional dishes are delightful with wonderful sounding names such as Disheen, Colcannon, Champ and Crubeens. They also have beautiful Limerick hams, succulent lamb and a wide variety of vegetables which grow in their fertile soil, the best know being the potato. Although not the oldest vegetable in Ireland, being introduced to Ireland by Sir Walter Raleigh in the 16th Century, it is easy to cultivate, therefore it soon became the mainstay of Irish cooking. Along with the vegetables and meat, the Irish have a wide range of cheeses. not forgetting, of course, their famous Guinness and Irish whiskey. The Irish have also made good use of the plentiful fish in their surrounding seas and the inland lakes and rivers.

Much of Irish cooking was roasting and boiling dating back to prehistoric times when a pit with an arc-shaped hearth at each end was built, called a "*fulachta fiadha*." The pit was filled with water and heated stones were put in which brought the water to boiling point. Large pieces of meat were wrapped in either hide or straw and tied with straw rope then lowered into the pits. It was found that a ten-pound leg of mutton cooked in three hours and forty minutes, which is twenty minutes to the pound and twenty minutes over; just as we cook roasts today. By this method meat was both roasted and boiled. A tradition carried on today at Christmas when the bird is roasted and the ham boiled.

In the past and today Irish soups play an important role. Most of them are simple and filling but with good flavour. During hard times the soups mainly consisted of water, potates and bacon, when available, but now they use plenty of fresh vegetables, meats and fish.

Vegetables are the most important ingredient in Irish cooking, and most country houses have their own vegetable garden. The true Irish flavour comes through with the combination of potatoes, cabbage, leeks and carrots mixed together with butter and cream. Not only do they make good use of fish in the surrounding waters, but also seaweed; Carrageen being the most popular for both a savoury and dessert dish. Not too many herbs are added to these simple dishes allowing their full flavour to come through.

The Dublin Bay prawn is the most famous of their fish. It is not really a prawn but a type of lobster and a relative of the Adriatic scampi. Here again, because of the good flavour of their fish very few sauces are needed. Herrings are very popular, along with mackerel, salmon, and Dover Sole. There are great oyster beds along the coast of Galway, which are best eaten fresh. Every year Galway has an oyster festival where the fastest oyster openers gather to try their skills.

With their lush green pastures there is no shortage of livestock. The Irish make full use of all of their animals using them in soups, main dishes and sausages.

Only the Irish would think of using the potato in bread and cake, but this was more out of necessity than being adventurous. Here again Irish breads and cakes are simple, but with a full flavour. Not only do they drink their Guinness and whiskey, but use it in their cakes giving them the typical flavour and also keeping the cakes moist.

WHAT'S THE DIFFERENCE

IRISH	AMERICAN
BAKING TRAY	COOKIE SHEET
BISCUITS	COOKIES or CRACKERS
BLACK TREACLE	MOLASSES
CORNFLOUR	CORNSTARCH
DRIPPING	MEAT DRIPPING
ESSENCE	EXTRACT
FARLS	QUARTERS
GLACE	CANDIED
GOLDEN SYRUP	LIGHT CORN SYRUP
GREASEPROOF PAPER	WAXED PAPER
GRILL	BROIL
HOUGH	SHANK OF BEEF
JAM or JELLY	PRESERVES
JELLY (SWEET)	GELATIN DESSERT, JELLO
PINHEAD OATMEAL	IRISH OATMEAL
RASHER OF BACON	SLICE OF BACON
RATAFIAS	ALMOND COOKIES or MACAROONS
SCONES	BISCUITS
SIEVE	SIFT
SELF-RAISING FLOUR	ALL-PURPOSE SELF-RISING FLOUR
SPRING ONIONS	SCALLIONS or GREEN ONIONS
SULTANAS	SEEDLESS WHITE RAISINS
WHISK	BEAT, WHIP

HINTS ON BAKING CAKES

Use a wooden spoon and a warm bowl to cream the margarine and sugar. Never allow the margarine to "oil."

Always break eggs separately into a cup. If one of them happens to be bad, this will prevent it spoiling the others.

Dip your spoon in milk before spooning the batter or mixture for small cakes. This will prevent the mixture sticking to the spoon.

Grease spoon before spooning syrup, this will help to prevent it sticking to the spoon.

Fruit, if washed, must be well dried before the cake is mixed. Damp fruit causes heaviness.

How to test if a large cake is sufficiently cooked:

a. When its surface is pressed lightly with a finger the cake should rise again, no impression being left.
b. A fine hot skewer (or thin steel knitting needle) inserted into the centre of the cake, should come out clean.
c. A slight sound of bubbling inside fruit cake indicates that the whole cake needs further cooking.

Always leave cakes a short while in the pan before turning them out, just long enough to "set," but not to cool. Then take them out and put to cool on a wire cooling tray.

CAKES KEEP BEST IN AN AIRTIGHT CONTAINER, BUT THEY MUST BE QUITE COOLED FIRST.

POTATO SOUP
Anraith prátaí

Although the potato is the most famous of all the Irish vegetables, it was not widely used until possibly the late 17th Century. Other vegetables and wild plants such as watercress and nettle have been eaten in Ireland for many centuries along with the onion family, such as the leek. A variety of carrot (meacan) has also been eaten in Ireland since early times. The potato, which was brought to Ireland in the 16th Century by Sir Walter Raleigh, has been much maligned probably because of the famine, but it makes an excellent soup and it can be a good basis for many other soups by the addition of different ingredients such as watercress, lobster, crab or prawns, or any cooked smoked fish.

2 lb. potatoes, peeled and diced
3 oz. butter
5 cups water
2 large onions, diced
3 tablsp. mixed dried herbs (such as parsley, thyme and sage)
2 tablsp. chopped chives or mint
salt and pepper to taste
1¼ cups milk
2 tablsp. cream

Melt the butter in a pan and slowly simmer the potatoes and onions. Do not brown. Add the water and herbs, salt and pepper and continue on a low heat until the vegetables are tender, for about half an hour. Remove from the heat and allow to cool. To make the soup really

1

smooth and creamy, put through a blender
before adding the cream and chives or mint.
Our grandmothers would not have done this but
it does give the soup a good texture. If you
do not blend the soup, serve very hot garnished
with the cream and chopped chives or mint.

Serves approximately 6

COCKLE SOUP
Anraith ruacan

Cockles are members of Cardium family and first
cousins of clams. They are very plentiful
along the western coast of Ireland and in Kerry
they are known as 'kirkeen' or 'carpetshell.'
Not only are cockles popular in soup but they
are also the subject of the traditional Irish
song "Cockles and Mussels."

In Dublin's fair city,
Where the girls are so pretty,
I first set my eyes on sweet
    Molly Malone,
As she wheel'd her wheelbarrow,
Through streets broad and narrow,
Crying, "Cockles and mussels alive,
    alive o!"

CHORUS:

Alive, alive o!
Alive, alive o!
Crying "Cockles and mussels
    alive, alive o!"

approximately 50 cockles
1 cup celery, chopped
2½ cups extra rich milk
2/3 cup cream
2 tablsp. butter
2 tablsp. flour
2 tablsp. parsley, chopped
salt and pepper to taste

Clean the cockles well and discard any that are open. Place in pan with salted water enough to just cover. Bring to the boil until they all open. Remove and let cool until they can be handled. Remove cockles and shell them, removing the beards, and keeping the strained liquid. Heat the flour and butter in a pan and blend in slowly, stirring all the time, the cockle liquid and extra rich milk, stirring until smooth. Add the chopped celery and cook for 5 minutes, then add the chopped parsley, salt and pepper to taste. Bring to the boil and then simmer for half an hour. Replace the cockles in the liquid and cook gently for a few minutes, until the cockles are heated through. Serve hot garnished with cream and a parsley sprig.

Serves approximately 4

MUSSEL SOUP
Anraith diúilicini

This soup can be made exactly the same as Cockle Soup substituting mussels for cockles.

4

TURNIP SOUP

3 large turnips, chopped
2 oz. butter
1 oz. flour
3 cloves
1 large onion, chopped
4 cups chicken stock
2 cups milk
1 teasp. sugar
salt and pepper to taste

Peel and chop the turnips and onion and add
to melted butter in a pan. Cover and cook
slowly for 30 minutes. Add the chicken stock
and cloves, cover and simmer for a further
30 minutes. Remove the cloves. Liquidize the
mixture and return to pan. Mix the flour to
a smooth paste with some of the milk and then
add to the soup with the remaining milk and
sugar. Season to taste and cook for a further
10 minutes.

LEEK AND OATMEAL SOUP

This is a very traditional soup which is some-times called brotchán foltchep or brachán rua. The Irish feel much the same about the 'leek' as their Welsh neighbours across the Irish Sea. The leek has been used in Ireland since early times, even before the potato, being an important ingredient in soup used in all Celtic countries.   The leek is also very prominent during Lent.

5-6 large leeks
5 cups milk
1/3 cup Irish Oatmeal
salt and pepper to taste
¼ oz of butter
¼ cup fresh parsley, chopped, for garnish

Wash the leeks thoroughly to remove all the dirt and trim the green ends. Cut leeks into 1 inch chunks, using both the green and white parts. Place milk and butter in pan and bring to the boil, add the oatmeal, and stir well. Bring to boil again after adding oatmeal, then lower heat and simmer about 20 minutes. Add leeks, salt and pepper to taste, and bring to the boil again. Lower heat and simmer until oatmeal is cooked--approximately 15 minutes. Serve hot garnished with chopped parsley.

Serves approximately 6

WATERCRESS SOUP
Anraith biolair

Watercress (biolair) grows all over Ireland in its clear unpolluted waters, and it is best picked in the spring.

2½ cups chicken stock
1¼ cups milk
1¼ cups cream
1 cup chopped celery
5 cups chopped watercress
2 tablsp. flour
2 tablsp. butter
salt and pepper to taste

Garnish:
2 tablsp. whipped cream
watercress leaflets

Place chicken stock, milk and cream in pan and gently simmer, add celery and simmer for 10 minutes. Remove from heat and leave covered to steep for half an hour. Heat butter and blend in flour and cook for 2 minutes, then slowly add the stock mixture stirring well, and cook for a further 5 minutes, stirring all the time until mixture is smooth and thick. Add salt and pepper to taste and the chopped watercress. If you wish the soup can be liquidized. Serve hot or cold garnished with the whipped cream and watercress leaflets.

Serves 4

NETTLE SOUP
Anraith neantóg

Nettle soup is very popular especially in the spring when the nettles are young and tender. The nettle contains a lot of iron and is said to improve the complexion. In the past they were given to children who had measles. The nettle leaves can raise blisters on the skin therefore gloves should be worn when gathering them. Cut the nettles with scissors and gather them before the end of May otherwise they will be tough.

If nettles are not available scallions (green onions) may be substituted for the nettles.

4 cups nettle leaves, chopped (or scallions)
1 cup pearl barley
1 lb potatoes, sliced
1 large leek, chopped
½ cup butter
4-1/3 cups chicken stock
2/3 cup cream
salt and pepper to taste

Heat the butter in a pan and then add the chopped nettles (or scallions) and leek, and cook for 5-10 minutes. Do not brown. Add the potatoes, pearl barley and stock. Simmer over a low fire for 1 hour. Liquidize the soup and then return it to the heat, season with salt and pepper to taste. Add the cream and serve hot.

Serves approximately 4-6

PEA SOUP
Anraith pise

Contrary to popular belief the pea is more popular in Ireland that the potato. They are eaten in all forms and are much used with corned pork or beef, and when mashed are called 'mushy' peas.   Dried peas make a good stock when boiled with bacon , ham, or pork.

1 lb green split peas, soaked 2-3 hours
1 ham bone
1 onion, chopped
6 cups water
1 bay leaf
1 sprig thyme
salt and pepper to taste
chopped parsley for garnish
crumbled bacon bits for garnish

Rinse the split peas and place in a pot with the coarsely chopped onion, cover with the water and add the ham bone and remaining herbs. Cover and bring to the boil. Lower heat and simmer until the peas 'are very soft. Remove the ham bone. Salt and pepper to taste.   If the soup is too thick add a little cream and bring back to almost boiling point. Serve hot garnished with chopped parsley and bacon bits.

Serves approximately 6

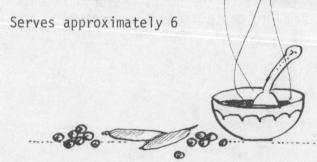

CRUBINS PEA SOUP
Anraith crubins pise

Crubins, also called crubeens, is the Irish name for pig's trotters.

1 lb dried green split peas, soaked 2-3 hours
8 cups water
3 pig's trotters
2 onions, chopped
1 whole celery, chopped
5 peppercorns
1 bay leaf
salt to taste
chopped parsley for garnish

Simmer the pig's trotters for 3 hours. Then add the remaining ingredients and simmer for a further hour. Remove the trotters from the pan and allow to cool. When cool remove the meat and cut in small pieces. Set aside. Put the vegetables and liquid through a sieve and then return to pot with the meat. Heat the soup and taste for seasoning. Serve hot garnished with chopped parsley.

Serves approximately 4-6

ONION SOUP
Anraith oinniún

In Ireland along with hot whiskey, onion soup is the cure for whatever ails you. This is a lovely creamy soup very different from the French brown onion soup.

1 lb onions, sliced
4-1/3 cups chicken stock
1-1/3 cups milk
2/3 cup cream
2 tablsp. butter
2 tablsp. flour
2 cloves
¼ teasp. nutmeg
1 bay leaf
salt and pepper to taste

Cook the onions and cloves in a pan with the butter until the onions are soft. Do not brown. Carefully add the flour, stirring well for 1 minute, then add the nutmeg, bay leaf and chicken stock. Bring to the boil stirring all the time until it is smooth. Lower heat and simmer until the onions are cooked, and then slowly add the milk and then the cream, stirring constantly. Remove the cloves and bay leaf. Serve hot garnished with grated cheese if desired.

Serves approximately 4

11

CLEAR SOUP
Anraith glé

Traditionally this clear soup is served as a first course to the Christmas dinner. This is delicious served with cheese biscuits. It can be served hot or cold, but if served cold it will be a soft jelly.

1 lb lean beef, sliced
1 lb. lean ham, sliced
1 veal knuckle or 1 split pig's foot
2 carrots, scraped and diced
2 onions, diced
2 heads of celery, chopped
1 bay leaf
2 tablsp. parsley, chopped
2 tablsp. thyme
10 cups water

Place all of the ingredients in a pan and bring to the boil. Reduce heat and simmer until the meat is tender. Strain through muslin. To clear beat two egg whites and stir in mixture. Return to heat and simmer for half an hour. Strain the liquid through muslin again and return to pan. Season with salt and pepper to taste. Serve hot or cold.

Serves approximately 10

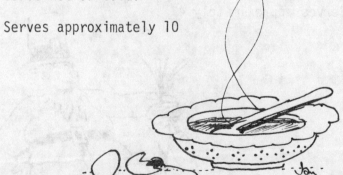

CARROT SOUP
Anraith meacan dearg

Carrots have been used in Ireland since pre-historic times. Carrots add sweetness to a meal and will also withstand long boiling in soups or stews.

4-1/3 cup chicken stock
1 leek or medium onion
6 medium carrots
1 tablsp. butter
1 garlic clove
¼ teasp. mace
2/3 cup cream
salt and pepper to taste
croutons for garnish

Clean carrots and cut into small pieces. Peel and chop the onion or leek and the garlic. Melt the butter in a pan and soften the vegetables in the butter. Do not brown. Add the stock and mace. Bring to the boil and then simmer for 1 hour, or until the vegetables are tender. Add salt and pepper to taste. Sieve or liquidize and return to the heat. Add the cream and heat gently. Do not boil. Serve hot garnished with croutons.

Serves approximately 4

CELERY SOUP
Anraith soilire

Wild celery was originally used in this soup but later when it was cultivated it became very popular for soups and sauces.

1 potato
1 medium onions
1 large head celery
1 clove garlic
1 tablsp. cornflour
¼ teasp. mace
7/8 cup cream
5 cups chicken stock
salt and pepper to taste
chopped parsley for garnish

Wash and chop the celery. Peel and chop the potato and onion. Melt the butter in a pan and gently cook the vegetables and minced garlic until they are soft. Do not brown. Cream the cornflour with 2 tablsp. stock and set aside. Heat the remaining stock and add the mace. Bring to the boil and then lower the heat and simmer the vegetables in the stock for about half an hour. Add salt and pepper to taste. Continue to simmer until the vegetables are well cooked, then add the creamed cornflour and stir until the soup returns to boiling point and thickens slightly. Sieve or liquidize and return to the saucepan, the add the cream and bring to just below boiling point. Do not boil. Serve hot garnished with chopped parsley.

Serves approximately 4-6

BROTH
Anraith

Broth is actually the liquid in which beef, mutton, chicken or bacon has been stewed with various vegetables and needs very long slow cooking. The meat can be removed from the broth and served separately, or can be cut in small pieces and replaced in the broth and served as a main course. It is believed that the pig was the first domesticated animal in Ireland which was used for broth. The broth was often drunk first and then the meat served as a second course with the vegetables. Dumplings can also be added for flavour and bulk, and can be made as follows:

DUMPLINGS
domplagáin

2 cups flour
1 egg
a little cold water to mix
salt to taste

Blend the egg with the flour and salt, and add enough water to make a stiff dough. Form into small balls and drop into the boiling broth 15 minutes before serving. Cover closely, and do not lift the lid until you are ready to serve to broth. Chopped parsley may also be added for extra flavour.

BEEF BROTH
Anraith mairteola

2 lb. beef, cubed
1 carrot
1 onion
1 turnip
½ small cabbage
1 tablsp. pearl barley
7½ cups water
2 oz. butter
salt and pepper to taste

Brown the beef in butter and then add water and seasoning, and simmer, covered, for 2 hours. Skim off all the fat and add pearl barley and chopped vegetables and continue to simmer for another hour. Taste for seasoning. Serve hot.

Serves approximately 6

MUTTON BROTH
Anraith caoireoil

This can be made the same as Beef Broth only substituting 2 lb. neck of mutton, cut into small pieces and trimmed of fat, in place of the beef.

BACON BROTH
Anraith bagúin

This can be made the same as Beef Broth only substituting 2 lb. shoulder of bacon (or ham) in place of the beef. You can also add 1 lb. peeled and sliced potatoes and 2 tablsp. lentils if desired.

EGG CUTLETS
Gearrthóga uibhe

*This is a very popular dish especially on
meatless days. It is commonly known as
Ulster eggs.*

3 cups mashed potatoes
3 hard-boiled eggs
1 tablsp. chives, chopped
1 tablsp. parsley, chopped
1 egg, beaten
½ teasp. ground nutmeg
2 tablsp. breadcrumbs
1 tablsp. brown flour
fat for frying

Shell the eggs and mash the whites and yolks
separately and then mix together. Combine
the potatoes, chives, nutmeg and parsley and
salt and pepper to taste. Mix in half the
egg mixture and a little flour to make a
firm consistency. Taste for seasoning.
Shape the mixture into cutlets and then dip
in the remaining egg mixture and then into
the breadcrumbs. Fry in hot fat until golden
on both sides.

Serves 4

SPICED BEEF
Mairteoil spíosraithe

This is a traditional Christmas dish which can be eaten hot or cold.

3 lbs. brisket of beef
1 cup coarse salt
1/3 cup brown sugar
¼ teasp. dry thyme
½ teasp. nutmeg
½ teasp. allspice
½ teasp. ground cloves
½ teasp. ground bay leaves
1 onion, finely chopped
2 oz. black treacle
freshly ground pepper
1 cup carrots, sliced

Rub the meat with the salt and leave overnight. Combine the nutmeg, allspice, sugar, cloves, pepper, bay leaves, and thyme. Rub the salt from the meat and dry. Rub the meat with the spice mixture, cover and refrigerate for 2 days. Heat the treacle and pour over the meat. Refrigerate overnight. Roll the meat and tie firmly. Place in a saucepan with enough water to cover it. Add the carrots and onions and simmer over a low heat for 3 hours. Cool the meat in the liquid. If desired 1 cup of Guinness may be added during the last hour of cooking. Serve cold and sliced.

Serves approximately 8

WICKLOW PANCAKE
Pancóg Chill Mhantáin

This is a very popular traditional dish and although called a 'pancake' it is somewhat of a misnomer as it is more like an omelette.

6 eggs
1 tablsp. parsley, chopped
2 tablsp. chopped chives or scallions
2 tablsp. butter
¼ teasp. thyme
½ cup breadcrumbs
2½ cup milk
salt and pepper to taste

Beat the eggs and then add the milk, bread-crumbs, herbs and seasonings. Mix well.
Heat 1 tablsp. butter in a pan until foaming.
Pour in the mixture and cook over a low flame until golden brown underneath and just set on top. Place under the grill to finish.
Serve in wedges with a knob of butter on each slice.

Serves approximately 4

TRADITIONAL PATE
Pâté Saibhir Tradisiúnta

1 lb chicken livers
4 eggs
4 egg yolks
3/4 cup flour
1 cup milk
½ teaps. nutmeg
1 teasp. chopped parsley
1 teasp. chopped basil
1 teasp. chopped tarragon
2 cloves crushed garlic
1 tablsp. butter
6 tablsp. whipped cream

Place the chicken livers in a blender and puree. Place in a bowl and gradually mix in the sieved flour. Mix well then add the eggs one at a time and then the yolks, one at a time. Add the milk, cream and salt and pepper to taste and all the herbs. Stir slowly with a wooden spoon until well blended. Grease a ring mould with butter and place the mixture in the mould. Place the mould in a baking tin filled with water and put in the oven for 1½ hours at 300. Check after the hour to see if there is enough water in the baking tin. Unmould and fill the centre with watercress. Serve with crackers.

CHAMP or STELK

This is very similar to Colcannon but chives or spring onions are used in place of cabbage. Champ is very traditional in the northern counties.

6-8 potatoes
1 cup chopped spring onions or
½ cup chopped chives
6-8 tablsp butter
1½ cups milk
salt and pepper to taste

If onions are used, cook until soft in the milk. Peel, cook and mash the potatoes and mix with the milk and onions or chives. Season to taste. Serve hot.

CALLY, POUNDIES or PANDY
Brúitín

Like Champ or Stelk which is popular in the northern counties, these three names are given to similar versions of the same dish which is popular in other parts of Ireland: mashed potatoes with onion, milk or cream, butter and seasoning.

BOXTY BREAD
Bacstaí

Boxty can be in the form of cakes, bread, pancakes, puddings and dumplings and is very traditional in the northern counties. It is often called "dippity" as Boxty was served with milk for dipping it in.

1 lb cooked mashed potatoes
1 lb raw potatoes, grated
1 lb flour
salt and pepper to taste
¼ cup bacon fat

Put the grated potatoes in a cloth and wring out as much liquid as possible. Save the liquid in a separate bowl. In another bowl put the grated potatoes, mashed potatoes, flour and salt and pepper. When the starch has sunk to the bottom of the bowl of liquid pour off the liquid from the top and put the starch into the other ingredients. Add the melted bacon fat and combine the ingredients throughly. Divide the mixture into four equal parts on a floured board and form them into flat round cakes. Make a cross on the top of the cakes. Place on a greased baking tray and bake in a preheated oven at 325, for 50 minutes. Serve hot splitting each cake into four and covering with butter.

Makes 4 cakes.

DUBLIN BAY PRAWNS
Piardóga

Dublin Bay Prawns are an Irish speciality, being very similar to the Adriatic scampi. They are not actually a prawn but a Norwegian lobster. They should be eaten freshly caught.

1 lb Dublin Bay Prawns
½ lb button mushrooms, sliced
2 oz butter
1 oz flour
1 cup cream
salt and pepper to taste
1 tablsp. Irish whiskey

Steam the prawns and then shell them. In a saucepan saute the mushrooms in the butter. Sprinkle the mushrooms with the flour and mix well. Lightly heat the cream and while continuously stirring pour it over the mushrooms and cook until creamy. Add the prawns and continue simmering for 4-5 minutes. Before serving, check seasoning, sprinkle the Irish whiskey over the prawns and serve with rice.

IRISH STEW
Stobhach Gaelach

Irish Stew is of course synonymous with Ireland and well-known throughout the Western world and is probably one of the oldest dishes in Ireland. Do you put carrots in your stew? You will get both a "yes" and "no" to this question. Some are of the theory that carrots are never added to a traditional Irish Stew and others will disagree. I believe the classic version does not contain carrots but it seems common practice in the south to use carrots. Another bone of contention is "barley." The recipe below does not include either carrots or barley, but they may be added if desired.

2 lb lamb neck chops
6 medium sized onions, chopped
2 lb. potatoes, peeled and sliced
2½ cups water
2 tablsp. parsley, chopped
salt and pepper

Put the meat at the bottom of a heavy, cast iron casserole and cover with a layer of chopped onions and then a layer of sliced potatoes. Add a little water and boil on top of the stove for 15 minutes. Add the remaining water, cover the casserole and place in the oven at 350, for 1 hour. Add the remaining onions and potatoes. Cover and return to the oven for a further hour, or until the vegetables are cooked and the meat tender. Serve directly from the casserole, garnished with parsley. If you prefer you can also cook the stew on top of the stove.
Simmer over a gentle heat, stirring occasionally, for 2 hours. Shake the pan from time to time to avoid sticking and add a very little water if necessary.

Serves approximately 4-6

SODA BREAD
Arán sóide

6 cups flour
¼ tablsp. salt
¼ tablsp. baking soda
1 cup buttermilk or sour milk

Mix all the dry ingredients together in a bowl
and then make a well in the centre. Stir in
the milk and mix thoroughly. If necessary add
a little more milk but do not make the mixture
too thin. Roll out the dough into a circle
about 1½ inches thick. Make a cross in the
dough. Place the dough on a baking sheet
and place in a preheated oven, 400, and bake
for approximately 40 minutes.

Brown Soda Bread may also be made by using
1 lb. wholewheat flour and ½ lb. plain white
flour. A little more milk may be needed to
mix the dough.

BUTTERMILK BREAD
Arán bláthaí

2 cups oatmeal
2 cups white flour
3 cups buttermilk
1 teasp. salt
1 teasp. baking soda
2 tablsp. brown sugar

Stir the buttermilk into the oatmeal, cover and
leave for 10-12 hours. Mix and then add the
remaining ingredients and perhaps a little more
buttermilk. Mix to a fairly stiff dough. Place
dough in two well-greased loaf tins and bake at
400 for 45 minutes. Test before removing from
the oven. Turn out and leave to cool covered
with a cloth.

25

SCALLOPS WITH MUSHROOMS
Camóga le beacáin

This is a very popular first course, made with
small scallops. In the west of Ireland they
are known as "queenies" or "closheens."

2 oz. button mushrooms, sliced
3 tablsp. olive oil
1 lb. scallops
1 large onion, sliced
juice of 1 lemon
1 tablsp. chopped parsley
salt and pepper

Place the scallops in boiling water for 2 mins.
Cool and set aside. Heat the oil and fry the
onions until soft, then add the mushrooms and
scallops. Cook until mushrooms are soft,
turning occasionally. Add the lemon juice,
salt, pepper and parsley.

Serves 4

CONVENT EGGS
Uibheacha clochair

This is an old recipe which Alexis Benoit Soyer, a French cook and writer on cookery, brought over with him when he visited Ireland to help provide food for the famine victims.

1 tablsp. butter, softened
4 eggs
salt and pepper to taste
4 tablsp. fresh heavy cream

Brush the insides of cocottes or ramekins with the butter. Break the eggs into the dishes, season with salt and pepper then spoon 1 tablsp. of cream over each egg. Place in a roasting tin half-full of water and cover the dishes with buttered greaseproof paper or foil. Bake in a moderate oven, 350, for 10 to 15 minutes or until eggs are set.

Serve immediately.

Chopped parsley or grated cheese may be sprinkled on top if desired.

CORNED BEEF AND CABBAGE
Mairteoil shaillte le cabáiste

This is probably the most famous of all Irish dishes being served on St. Patrick's Day and also during the winter months.

3 lbs corned beef, soaked overnight to remove
                    excess salt
2 carrots, sliced
2 onions, chopped
3 stalks celery, chopped
4 bay leaves
2 sprigs parsley, chopped
2 sprigs thyme, chopped
6 peppercorns
1 large cabbage cut into 6-8 pieces

In a large saucepan combine all of the ingredients except the cabbage. Cover with water and bring to a slow boil. Lower heat and simmer for 1 hour. If necessary take off any scum that may form on top. Add the cabbage and cover, simmer for a further 2 hours. When cooked, remove the meat and allow to sit for 10 minutes, then slice and serve surrounded by the cabbage and vegetables.

Serves approximately 6-8

TRIPE AND ONIONS
Tríopas agus ionníuin

This is a very popular Saturday night dinner which is usually served with sliced onions and, of course, a pint of Guinness.

2 lb tripe, cut into 2 inch pieces
3 cups milk
1 cup water
3 slices bacon, roughly chopped
6 onions, sliced
3 tablsp. flour
1 tablsp. parsley, chopped
½ cup breadcrumbs
1 oz butter, melted
salt and pepper to taste

In a casserole mix the tripe, bacon, onions, milk, water and salt and pepper. Cover and bring to the boil, then reduce heat and simmer for 2 hours. Mix the flour in a little of the cooking liquid and then mix into the tripe. Cover and simmer for a further 30 minutes. Add the parsley, sprinkle with breadcrumbs and pour over the melted butter. Brown under the grill.

Serves approximately 6-8

DONEGAL PIES
Pióga Donegal

½ lb. Rough Puff Pastry
½ lb. bacon
2 hardboiled eggs
2 lb. mashed potatoes

Grease a pie dish and half fill with the
potatoes. Slice the eggs and place them on
top. Fry the bacon until crisp, then sprinkle
on top of the eggs and pour over the bacon fat.
Cover with the remaining potatoes. Prepare
the pastry, roll out and cover the pie dish.
Bake in a hot oven, 375, for 1 to 1½ hours.

PORK CÍSTE
Císte muiceola

The name 'císte' may be confusing as it can also mean cake as well as pudding. This is a very old traditional dish but not made that often today. It can be made with lamb or mutton.

6 pork chops, trimmed of fat
2 pork kidneys
1 large onion, sliced
1 large carrot, sliced
2 cups flour
1 cup suet, grated
½ cup milk
3 tablsp. sultanas, optional
1 tablsp. parsley, chopped
2¼ cups stock
¼ teasp. thyme
salt and pepper to taste
1 teasp. baking soda

Place the chops around the edge of a flame-proof dish. Then to the centre add the pork kidney, sliced, along with the vegetables and herbs. Season and add enough stock to just cover the vegetables. Cover, bring to the boil, and then lower heat and simmer for half an hour. Make the 'císte' by mixing the flour, salt, suet and baking soda and enough milk to make a firm dough. Add sultanas if used. Mix well and then roll out on a floured board. Roll the pastry to the size of the pan. Place the pastry on top of the pan and then press down until it is about 1 inch from the vegetables. If the chops stick through the pastry it does not matter. Cover with greased wax paper and then place the lid on top and cook for 1-1½ hours over a low heat.

Serves 4-6

CREAMED CABBAGE
Cabaiste le hanlann uachtair

Cabbage is probably the most used vegetable in Ireland and this is a popular dish in the Tipperary area.

1 cabbage (about 2 lbs.)
2¼ cups light cream
¼ teasp. nutmeg
2 tablsp. butter
2 tablsp. flour
salt and pepper to taste

Clean the cabbage and cut into about 8 pieces. Blanch in salted boiling water for about 5 mins. Drain well and cut into thin strips. Heat the butter and then stir in the flour and cook for 1 minute. Gradually add the milk and nutmeg, stirring well to avoid lumps. Add the cabbage and bring to the boil. Cover and cook over a low heat for 15 minutes, stirring occasionally. Serve when the cabbage is still firm.

Serves approximately 4

BRAISED GOOSE
Gé ghalstofa

Goose was always the bird used on festive occasions in Ireland but it has now been replaced by the turkey since the turn of the century. The goose was either boiled or braised and most homes did not have an oven. Over the fire they would hang a large pot and do all of their cooking in this pot. Which might account for the saying "to take pot luck." An old tradition is that if you eat goose on Michaelmas Day, September 29th, you will have good luck for the whole year.

1 goose, about 10 lbs. (jointed)
2 tablsp. goose fat
6 medium carrots, sliced
2 onions, stuck with cloves
3 parnips, chopped
1 head celery, chopped
¼ teasp. sage
seasoned flour
4 cups giblet stock

Clean and wipe the goose and prick all over with a fork. Roll the goose in the seasoned flour. Heat the goose fat and brown the joints all over. Transfer to fat to a larger pot and brown the vegetables in the same fat. Put in the remainder of the goose and sprinkle with the sage. Heat the stock and pour it over the goose and vegetables and bring to the boil, lower heat and cover simmering for about 1½ hours. Dumplings may be added to the goose and then cooked for a further half hour.

Serves 10-12

STEAK WITH WHISKEY
Steig le hUisce beatha

*This is not strictly a traditional Irish dish
but it is becoming more popular and is quite
often referred to as "Gaelic Steak."*

Using one steak per person, cook the fillet
of steak in a little butter in a very hot pan.
When cooked as desired pour 2 tablsp. warmed
Irish whiskey over the meat and set alight.
Remove from pan and place on a warmed dish.
Add 3 tablsp. cream to the pan juices and mix
well. Boil to reduce the mixture a little
and then pour over the steaks. Serve at once
garnished with watercress.

34

WATER BISCUITS
Brioscaí uisce

Water biscuits are thin and flaky and usually
served with cheese. The story is that they
were first made in the late 1800s in Waterford
by William Jacob and his brother who immigrated
to Ireland. We do not know how true this story
is but Jacobs Cream Crackers are still well-
known throughout the world.

4 cups flour
2 tablsp. butter
a little less than 2/3 cup milk
¼ teasp. salt

Sift the flour and salt together. Heat the
milk and melt the butter in the milk. Add
the flour and mix well to make a smooth dough.
Roll out thinly on a floured board and cut
into 3 inch rounds. Place on a lightly
greased baking tray, and prick all over with
a fork. Bake at 400 for 10 minutes or until
they are crisp and light golden brown.

IRISH HUNTER'S PIE

1 onion, finely chopped
2 stalks celery, finely chopped
1 carrot, finely chopped
2 oz. butter
1-3/4 cups beef stock
6 lamb chops
3 lb. mashed potatoes
salt and pepper to taste

Melt half the butter and saute the onions,
carrot, onion and celery. Do not brown. Add
the stock and place the chops on top of the
vegetables. Cover and cook over a low heat
for 30 minutes. Remove the chops from the pan
and put the vegetables and liquid through a
sieve. Reserve the liquid. Place two-thirds
of the potatoes in a buttered pie dish and then
place the chops on top. Season and cover with
the remaining potatoes. Dot the top with the
remaining butter and bake in a preheated oven
at 400, until brown. Make a hole in the top
of the potatoes and pour in some of the vegetable liquid. Serve the remaining liquid with
the pie.

Serves approximately 6

MUTTON PIES
Pióga caoireola

These pies are similar to Cornish pasties commonly known as 'Dingle Pies.' To this day they are still sold in Dingle and you cannot go to the Puck Fair held every August in Killorglin without having a 'Dingle Pie.'

Rough Puff Pastry
2 lb lean mutton (lamb may be used if
                mutton is not available)
1 onion, finely chopped
2 teasp. fresh mint, chopped
¼ teasp. thyme
salt and pepper to taste

Prepare the pastry and then roll out on a floured board and cut 6 circles about 4 inches in diameter and 6 circles slightly smaller. Cut the mutton in small pieces and then add the onion, mint, thyme and salt and pepper to taste. Divide the mixture evenly between the 6 larger circles. Dampen the edges of the circles and then place the smaller circles on top of the mixture. Press down and crimp the edges with a fork. Make a small slip in the top of each 'Dingle' and then brush with a little milk. Place on a greased baking sheet and put in the oven at 350, for 15 minutes. Lower the heat to 325 and cook for a further 45 minutes. If you use raw meat the pies may need a further 15-20 minutes.

Makes 6 pies

BLACK PUDDING
Putóga fola

Most Celtic countries have a black pudding which
is sometimes referred to as "blood Pudding."
It was originally made with sheep's blood but
nowadays pig's blood is used. A similar dish
to Black Pudding is "Drisheen" which is traditional around Cork. White pudding is also
very similar made with finely minced boiled liver
and without the blood. These puddings are
sliced and fried and served as a part of
breakfast.

5 cups pig's blood
1½ cups breadcrumbs
1 cup suet
5 cups milk
1 cup cooked barley
1 cup dry oatmeal
1 oz mint (optional)
salt and pepper to taste

Mix all the ingredients together in a bowl then
pour into a large pan and bring to the boil.
Pour into a wide shallow bowl and season again
if necessary. Allow to cool. When cold it may
be cut into slices and fried.

Serves approximately 8

DUBLIN CODDLE
Codal Duibhlinneach

This has been a popular dish in Ireland since the 18th Century, mixing two of Ireland's much used foods.

6 thick bacon slices
6 pork sausages
3 large onions, sliced
1½ lb. potatoes, peeled and sliced
3 tablsp. chopped parsley
4 cups boiling water
salt and pepper to taste

Boil the bacon and sausages in the water for 5 minutes and then drain and reserve the water. On top of the bacon and sausages place layers of onions and potatoes and the chopped parsley. Season lightly. Cover with the liquid. Cover the saucepan and place in a preheated oven at 300, for 1 hour, or until the ingredients have cooked through but are not soft.

Serve hot with soda bread and Guinness.

Serves approximately 6

PIG'S TROTTERS CRUBEENS
Crúibíní

This is very much a country dish and is usually eaten with soda bread and a pint of Guinness.

12 pig's trotters
3 tablsp. chopped parsley
3 carrots, sliced
3 onions, chopped
3 bay leaves
½ teasp. thyme
3 stalks celery, chopped
6 peppercorns
2 eggs lightly beaten
¼ teasp. English mustard
breadcrumbs
salt
dripping, or cooking fat

Combine the trotters, onions, carrots, celery, peppercorns, bay leaves, thyme, parsley and salt in a large saucepan. Add enough water to cover. Bring to the boil, reduce the heat and simmer for 2½ hours or until the meat is tender. Remove the trotters from the liquid and pull the meat from the bones. Strain and reserve the liquid for later use as stock. Dust the meat with flour, dip in the mixture of egg and mustard and coat in breadcrumbs. Heat the dripping or cooking fat and fry the meat until brown and crisp. Serve hot with Michael Kelly's sauce.

Serves approximately 6

MICHAEL KELLY'S SAUCE

This sauce can be served with Crubeens,
boiled tongue, or tripe.   Michael Kelly
was an Irish composer who was born in
Cork around 1790.

1 tablsp. brown sugar   1 cup butter
1 teasp. black pepper
1 teasp. mustard powder
2 tablsp. garlic vinegar

Mix together with brown sugar, pepper and
mustard and then stir in the garlic vinegar.
Blend well then stir in melted butter and
stir until well mixed.

SPATCHCOCK
Éan luathbhruite

Spatchcock comes from 'dispatch cock' which is to kill a bird and cook it in a hurry, and is a very old method of cooking chicken.

12 small onions
12 button mushrooms
½ oz butter
1 clove garlic, crushed
2 spatchcocks 1¼ lb each (Cornish hen may be
                                        used)
1 cup cubed ham
3 sprigs marjoram, chopped
2 cups ale (beer)
salt and pepper to taste
8 deep fried bread slices
chopped parsley for garnish

Saute the onions and mushrooms in butter, then add the spatchcocks, ham, garlic, marjoram, salt, pepper and salt. Cover and cook over a low heat for 45 minutes, or until the spatchcocks are tender. Cut each bird in half and place on the deep fried bread which has been cut into croutons, and sprinkle with parsley.

BEEF OLIVES

This is an old 18th Century recipe probably brought over to Ireland from France. Thin slices of pork, ham or corned beef may be used in place of steak if desired.

12 thin slices of steak (about 1 lb.)
1 onion, finely chopped
2 egg yolks
2 tablsp. cooking fat
flour
2½ cups beef stock
2 tablsp. breadcrumbs
grated rind of 1 lemon
1 tablsp. chopped parsley

Beat the slices of steak to flatten them as much as possible. Combine onion, lemon rind, parsley, breadcrumbs, and egg yolks. Mix well, add salt and pepper if necessary. Place a small amount of the mixture on each slice of beef and roll up tightly, securing with a cocktail stick. Heat the oil and then saute the "olives". Drain off excess fat, sprinkle with flour and cook for another minute, add the stock and bring to the boil. Place in an ovenproof dish, cover and cook for 40 minutes, until tender, stirring occasionally. Transfer to a dish and serve with creamed potatoes and a vegetable. Remove the cocktail sticks from the "olives" before serving.

Serves approximately 4

COLCANNON
Cál ceannann

Colcannon is a traditional dish in most of the Celtic countries. In Scotland it is called Colcannon or Kailkenny and on the Borders a similar dish is called Rumbledethumps. Traditionally Colcannon is eaten at Hallowe'en. The name comes from cal ceann fhionn - white headed cabbage. Colcannon is correctly made with Kale, but cabbage can be substituted if Kale is not available. At Hallowe'en a gold ring, a sixpence, a thimble and a button were placed in the Colcannon. The person who found the ring meant they would be married within the year, the sixpence meant wealth, the thimble meant spinsterhood and the button bachelorhood.

6-8 potatoes
1 head of cabbage or kale
1½ cups milk
6-8 tablsp. butter
salt and pepper to taste

Peel, cook and mash the potatoes. Quarter, core and finely shred the cabbage. Cook the cabbage, but do not overcook. Stir the cabbage into the mashed potatoes, adding the butter, milk and salt and pepper to taste. Heat immediately and them serve in a warm dish, hollowing the centre a little and placing a small amount of butter in the hollow to melt into the vegetables.

COD WITH COCKLES
Trosc le ruacáin

This is a very traditional Galway dish. If cod is not available any white fish may be used. If cockles are not available they may be substituted with Clams.

2 lb cod
25 cockles
1 sprig fresh thyme or ½ teasp. dried thyme
4 tablsp. butter
6 boiling onions, parboiled
10 new potatoes, parboiled
1 tablsp. parsley, chopped
salt and pepper to taste
lemon wedges for garnish

Clean cockles and place in pan with water to cover. Bring to the boil and then shake for a few minutes. Strain, reserving the juice. When cockles have cooled, shell them.
Place cod in well-buttered overproof dish and season with salt and pepper and thyme. Place the parboiled onions and potatoes around the fish and then pour the cockles and strained cockle juice over the cod. Melt the remaining butter and pour over the fish. Cover with foil and bake at 400 for 25 minutes. Garnish with parsley and lemon wedges.

Serves approximately 4

POTTED CRAB
Portán potáin

"Potting" is a very old method of preserving fish, meat and poultry other than by smoking or salting. Spices were added and the butter covered and sealed the fish for many months giving the people fresh fish in the middle of the winter.

½ cup butter
juice of 1 lemon
1 lb. crabmeat
½ cup butter
¼ teasp. mace
salt and pepper

Mash the crabmeat and then mix throughly with the lemon juice, butter, mace and salt and pepper. Place in small pots, pressing down well in the corners, then cover thickly with clarified butter. Chill.

Serves 4

FADGE

Fadge is the northern Irish name for potato cake. It is also similar to Milk Fadge in the north of England where they omit the potatoes and use flour.

2 lbs. mashed potatoes
4 tablsp. flour
salt
2 tablsp. butter
bacon fat

Mix the butter with the mashed potatoes and then work in the flour. Mix well. Add more flour if they are not of a floury consistency. Add the salt to taste. Roll out on a floured surface to about ½ inch thick and then cut into large rounds. Prick the cakes on both sides and cook on a griddle about 3 minutes each side.

Makes about 10-12 cakes

You can store these cakes in an airtight tin for later use. They are usually served with eggs and bacon for breakfast.

SCONES
Bonnóga

½ cup margarine
4 cups flour
1/3 cup sugar
1 egg yolk mixed with a little cold water
milk
pinch of salt

Sift the flour and salt in a bowl and then
rub in the margarine. Add the sugar and then
the milk, a little at a time, until it is a
soft consistency. Roll out on a floured
board until it is about 3/4 inch thick. Cut
into rounds about 2½ inches in diameter
and place on a greased baking sheet. Brush
with the egg yolk and water mixture and then
place in preheated oven, 375, and bake for
20 minutes or until golden brown. Remove
from the oven and cool on a wire rack.

Makes approximately 15 scones

48

POTATO SCONES
Bonńoga prátaí

8 oz. cold mashed potatoes
½ cup oatmeal
½ teasp. baking soda
½ oz. butter, melted
½ teasp. salt

Mix the butter, salt and potatoes together. Add
the oatmeal and baking soda and mix into a
pliable dough. Roll out the dough, keeping it
fairly thick, and cut into circles, approximately
7-8 inches in diameter. Prick on top with a fork
and score into farls (quarters), without cutting
right through. Cook on a hot griddle for 4 mins
each side. Serve hot with butter.

BOILED CAKE
Císte beirithe

1/3 cup golden syrup
½ cup sugar
½ cup butter
2 cups flour
1 teasp. mixed spice

2/3 cup water
3/4 cup sultanas
3/4 cup currants
3/4 teasp. baking soda
1 egg, beaten

In a pan combine water, sugar, syrup, currants,
sultanas and butter. Heat for 10 minutes
stirring constantly. Allow to cool. Mix
together the flour, baking soda and spice and
stir in the liquid. Mix in the egg. Pour the
dough into a well-greased 8 inch baking tin and
bake at 350 for 1½ to 2 hours. Test before
taking out of oven.

APPLE BRACK
Bairín úll

This is a very traditional cake which is eaten
at Hallowe'en. It can be made ahead of time
and kept for a month in an airtight tin.

4 cup flour
1 cup butter
1 cup sultanas
2 teasp. baking soda
1 cup raisins
1-1/3 cup cooked apple
1 egg
a little milk

Rub the butter into the sifted flour and baking
soda. Add the sultanas and raisins and mix
well. Add the cooked apple. Beat the egg with
a little milk and add to the mixture. Mix well.
Place in an 8 inch cake tin and bake in oven at
375 for approximately 1½ hours.

IRISH TREACLE LOAF

2 oz butter   1/3 cup raisins
2 oz black treacle   1/3 cup currants
2 oz brown sugar   ½ teasp. mixed spice
1/3 cup water   ½ teasp ground ginger
1 egg   1 teasp. baking soda
2 cups flour

Preheat oven to 350. Heat the water and melt
the butter in it. Mix the treacle with the
sugar and egg until creamy. Mix the flour,
ginger, spice and baking soda and add to the
treacle mixture. Stir in the currants, raisins
and water/butter mixture. Pour the dough into
a 2 lb. bread tin and bake for 1½ to 2 hours.

BURNT ORANGES
Oráistí dóite

1-1/3 cup freshly squeezed orange juice
4 teasp. sugar
1 teasp. butter
4 large oranges
2 tablsp. Irish whiskey
2/3 cup sweet white wine
4 tablsp. sugar

Peel the oranges being careful to remove
the pith and white skin. Keep the oranges
intact. Cut the peel into fine strips and
cover with the wine. Place the oranges in
an ovenproof dish. Place a little butter
on top of each then sprinkle each with
a teasp. of sugar. Place in a 400 oven for
10 minutes until the sugar caramelizes. In
another bowl mix the orange juice with the
sugar (4 tablsp.) in a pan and bring to the
boil. Add the orange peel and wine and
bring to the boil again. Cook rapidly
until the mixture has thickened slightly.
Remove the oranges from the oven and pour
the warmed whiskey over them and set
alight. As the flames die down add the
orange syrup and let simmer for about 2
minutes. Serve at once.

Serves 4

BARM BRACK
Bairín breac

This is a traditional cake eaten at Hallowe'en
when a ring is included with the ingredients.
Whoever gets the ring will be married within
a year.

3½ cup flour
pinch of salt
½ oz fresh yeast
1 teasp. mixed spice
1 teasp. sugar
1¼ cup warm water
6 tablsp. butter
3/4 cup currants
3/4 cup raisins
3/4 cup sultanas
2 tablsp. candied peel
2 eggs
½ cup sugar

For Glaze:
2 tablsp. sugar
1 teasp. water

Cream the yeast with a teasp. of sugar. Add
the water. Sieve flour with salt and spice and
mix to a stiff dough with the yeast mixture.
Knead until smooth and springy; about 5 mins.
Leave in a bowl covered with a cloth in a warm
place for 1 hour, or until it has doubled in
size. Add the beaten eggs, fruit, sugar and
melted butter. Beat well. Half fill two
greased bread tins with the mixture and put
back to rise in a warm place, covered with a
cloth. Leave for approximately 1 hour to rise
to the top of the tins. Preheat oven to 375 .
Bake the bracks for approximately 50 minutes,
until fairly firm and brown. Dissolve 2 tablsp.

of sugar in 4 teasp. water over heat, boil for ½ minute, then brush this glaze over the bracks as you take them out of the oven.

OATCAKES
Bonnóga arán coirce

Oatcake are probably the oldest and most traditional of all Irish foods. Originally oatcakes were cooked on a griddle and then allowed to cool and harden on a 'hardening' stand.

2 cups oatmeal
1 teasp. salt
1 cup flour, sifted
1 teasp. baking soda
2 tablsp. butter

Mix the oatmeal with the flour, salt and baking soda. Make a well in the mixture. Heat 2 tablsp. water and add the butter; bring to the boil and then pour into the well of dry ingredients. Quickly mix together. Knead lightly and add a little more water if the mixture does not form a stiffish dough. Roll out and cut into 3 inch rounds and cook on both sides on a heated griddle, or bake on a lightly greased baking tray at 350 for half an hour or until golden in colour. Makes approximately 15 oatcakes.

Griddle or
Girdle

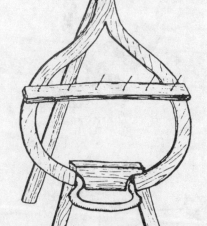

Hardening Rack
or Bake Stick

GUINNESS CAKE
Ciste Guinness

½ cup butter
1½ cup brown sugar
3 cups flour
pinch of salt
3 eggs, lightly beaten
¼ teasp. mixed spice
1/3 cup mixed peel
½ cup raisins
1 cup sultanas
1/3 cup glacé cherries
½ cup Guinness

Cream the butter and sugar until sugar has dissolved and then add the beaten eggs and flour, salt, mixed spice and dried fruit to the butter/sugar mixture. Finally mix in the Guinness. Pour the mixture into a well-greased cake tin and place in the pre-heated 350 oven and bake for 2 hours. Test before taking out. Remove from oven and allow to cool.

APPLE BARLEY FLUMMERY
Boighreán úll

Although not very popular today, this is an extremely old recipe. Apples can be replaced with gooseberries or blackcurrants or any other fairly soft fruit if you wish.

1/3 cup sugar
juice of 1 lemon
4 tablsp. pearl barley
1½ lb. eating apples, peeled, cored and sliced
1 teasp. heavy cream

Place the pearl barley in 4½ cups water and bring to the boil. Add the sliced apples and cook gently until the barley is soft. Put the mixture through a sieve or liquidize and put back in the pan. Add the sugar and lemon juice and bring to the boil. Remove from the heat and allow to cool. Then chill. Serve with the cream stirred in.

Serves approximately 4

BURNT SUGAR SAUCE
Anlann siúcra dhóite

This is a very old recipe when rich desserts were very popular. It can be served as a cream over fruit or over ice cream.

2/3 cup sugar
1-1/3 cup heavy cream

Place the sugar in a pan over a moderate heat and stir until the sugar melts and turns a golden brown. Remove from heat. Add 8 tablsp. cold water at once. Hold pan away from you as it will boil and sputter immediately the water is added. Place over a gentle heat and stir until it is a thin caramel liquid. Pour into a basin and leave to cool. Whip the cream very lightly and add the cold caramel to the whipped cream stirring until smooth and creamy.

Serves approximately 6-8

PORTER PUDDING
Maróg phórtair

Porter is not quite as strong as Guinness and can be difficult to find. If you use Guinness, halve the quantity.

1-3/4 cup flour
2 cup breadcrumbs
½ cup sultanas
½ cup currants
½ cup chopped peel
grated rind 1 orange and 1 lemon
1½ oz. Irish whiskey
1-1/3 cup porter (1 cup Guinness)
1 teasp. cinnamon
2/3 cup brown sugar
6 eggs

Place the sultanas, chopped peel, currants, lemon and orange rind, whiskey and porter in a bowl and mix well. Cover and leave overnight. The next day add the remaining ingredients and mix well. Place in a well greased basin and cover with greaseproof paper and then foil and tie with string. Steam for 3 hours. Serve hot with brandy sauce.

BRANDY SAUCE
Anlann brandaí

½ cup butter
1 cup confectioner's sugar
1 teasp. vanilla essence
6 tablsp. brandy
1 cup heavy cream

Stir the butter and confectioner's sugar over heat. Permit to boil. Remove at once, add brandy and vanilla essence. Whip the cream and fold mixture into cream. Stir well. This sauce may be served hot or cold.

GUINNESS CHRISTMAS PUDDING
Maróg Guinness Nollag

The Christmas Pudding became popular during the 19th Century. Before then a plain boiled fruit pudding was served. This pudding should be made no later than the beginning of November; they will keep in an airtight tin for up to a year.

1 cup flour
2 cups soft breadcrumbs
1-2/3 cup sultanas
½ cup glace cherries
1 cup raisins
½ cup mixed peel
1¼ cup brown sugar
1 cup chopped suet
3/4 cup Guinness
pinch of mixed spice
pinch of cinnamon
pinch of salt
5-7 eggs

Combine all dry ingredients in a large mixing bowl, then add the fruit. Stir in the well beaten eggs and then the Guinness. Grease 2 7 inch cooking basins and pour the mixture into them. Cover with foil and tie down with string. Steam the puddings 4 to 5 hours. Allow puddings to cool. Store in a dry cupboard in a tightly sealed tin. When used, steam the pudding for 3 hours before serving. Traditionally this pudding is served with Irish Whiskey Butter.

IRISH WHISKEY BUTTER
Im uisce beatha

2 tablsp. Irish whiskey
2 oz. butter
½ cup powdered sugar

Cream the sugar and butter until the sugar
is dissolved, then gradually add the whiskey.
Refrigerate and serve with the pudding which
has been flamed with Irish whiskey.

DUBLIN ROCK
Carraig Dhuibhlinneach

This is a very rich pudding popular during the 19th Century. It was usually decorated with angelica and sliced almonds to resemble a rocky plant.

1-2/3 cup heavy cream
1 cup ground almonds
1 tablsp. brandy
2 egg whites, stiffly beaten
½ cup unsalted butter
½ cup castor sugar
few drops of orange flower water

Cream the butter and sugar, then add the whipped cream. Fold in the ground almonds very gently. Add the orange flower water and brandy, then the stiffly beaten egg whites. Pour the mixture in a dish and refrigerate to set. Remove and break into rough size pieces and pile high on a platter. Decorate as desired.

POTATO AND APPLE CAKE
Cácá prátai agus úll

This is a very traditional cake in Ireland where there is an abundance of good apples. It was especially popular in last century with the country folk.

1 lb. potatoes
2 lb. cooking apples, peeled, cored and sliced
4 oz. flour
1 tablsp. brown sugar
2 teasp. sugar
pinch of ground ginger
1 oz. butter

Boil the potatoes and mash well, making sure there are no lumps. Mix in the flour, butter, sugar and ginger and knead to make a pliable dough, but not too much as this will toughen it. Roll out into a circle and place the apples on one half. Fold the other half on top and pinch round to seal. Put on a greased baking sheet and cover with the brown sugar. Cut a small vent and prick all over lightly. Brush with milk and bake at 375 for 40 minutes, or until the top is golden and the apples cooked. Remove from oven and peel back the top and add a knob of butter and more brown sugar. Keep hot until the butter and sugar have combined. Cut in slices and serve hot.

Serves approximately 4

PORRIDGE
Brachán

Traditionally porridge is served with a pinch of salt, but nowadays most people use sugar to sweeten it. (My father would never have agreed with the use of sugar.) Porridge has been the mainstay in most Celtic countries for many many years.

Allow for each serving:

1 cup water
1/3 cup oatmeal
1/8 teasp. salt

Bring the water to boil and add the salt. Sprinkle the oatmeal slowly into the boiling water, stirring constantly. Half cover the pan and turn the heat down to low. Stir occasionally until porridge thickens and is creamy - about 30 minutes. Add more salt if desired.

GUR CAKE
Gur-císte

During the poor times in Ireland in the 19th
and early 20th Centuries, this was a popular
cake. It was cheap and the bakers could use
their stale cake or bread stocks.

½ lb. stale bread, without crusts, or cake
2 oz. flour
2 oz. milk
1 egg
½ teasp. baking soda
2 teasp. mixed spice
6 oz. currants or mixed dried fruit
2 oz. brown sugar
2 tablsp. butter
8 oz. shortcrust pastry
sugar for sprinkling

Soak the bread in a little water for an hour,
then squeeze out the excess water. (Soak cake
the same if used.) Combine all the dry
ingredients with the egg and milk. Roll out
the pastry, cut in two and line the base of
a 9 inch square tin. Spread the mixture
evenly on top, and cover with the rest of the
pastry. Make a few diagonal cuts across the
top and bake at 375 for half an hour. Sprinkle
the top with sugar and allow to cool. Cut into
squares.

YELLOWMAN

Yellowman is a brittle texture toffee which has been made by the same family in Ireland for several hundred years. It is always a tradition to have a piece of Yellowman at the Lammas Fair, Ballycastle, Co. Antrim, on the last Tuesday in August.

Lammas-tide is a very ancient holiday which eventually became the original August Bank Holiday. There are various theories as to the origin of the word 'Lammas.' One is that it was derived from 'Lamb Mass' in ancient times when the tithe lambs were presented to the church. Another is that 'Lammas' derived from the Anglo-Saxon word 'hlafmaesse' which means 'loaf mass.' This was a feast where bread was made from the first corn of the year's harvest. Another connection is with the ancient Celtic Quarter Day of Lugnasad. Lugh was an important Celtic god, and is commemorated in several place names in Celtic Countries. Lugnasad also seems to be a festival marking the start of the harvest.

Lammas-tide was also a great time for fairs, especially sheep fairs.

1 lb. golden syrup (light corn syrup)
1 lb. brown sugar
¼ lb. butter
1 teasp. baking soda
2 tablsp vinegar

Dissolve the sugar, butter, syrup and vinegar in a well-greased shallow pan. Bring to a boil and stir until all ingredients are

melted. Boil until a drop hardens in cold
water. Remove from the heat and quickly stir
in the baking soda which will foam up. Stir
again and then pour on a greased slab and pull
the toffee when cool enough to handle, until
it is a pale yellow, then pour into a greased
dish and mark in squares. Cool and break into
squares and store in an airtight tin.

SEED CAKE
Cácá cearbhais

*Seed cake is a very old cake commonly known as
'carvie cake.'*

4 eggs
1 tablsp. caraway seeds
2 cups flour
4 tablsp. milk
1 cup sugar and 1 cup butter

Cream the butter and sugar and beat in the eggs
one at a time. Sift the flour and add slowly
to the mixture. Then add the caraway seeds.
Add the milk to make a soft mixture. Place in
an 8 inch cake tin and bake in a preheated oven
at 325 for 1½ hours. Test before taking out.
Leave in the tin for 15 minutes then remove and
place on a wire rack to cool.

PORTER CAKE
Ciste pórtair

Porter Cake is not quite as rich as the
Christmas Cake. It can be iced for
Christmas and plain at other times of the
year. It can be made at least a week
ahead and kept in an airtight tin.

4 cup flour
1 cup butter
1 cup raisins
1 cup currants
½ cup mixed peel
grated rind of 1 lemon
2 cups brown sugar
1-2/3 cup porter (Guinness may be used if
                  porter not available)
1 teasp. baking soda
2 teasp. mixed spice
4 eggs, well beaten

Rub the flour and butter together then add
the currants, raisins, mixed peel, lemon
rind and sugar. Mix well. Warm the porter
then pour over to baking soda and stir.
Add the beaten eggs to the mixture and
gradually stir this into the flour and fruit
mixture. Beat well. Pour mixture into a
well-greased 9 inch cake tin, cover loosely
with greaseproof paper and bake in a preheated oven at 325 for 1 hour, then lower
the heat to 300 and bake for a further 2
hours. Test before taking out. Allow to
cool in the tin. Store in an airtight tin
about a week before cutting.

TIPSY CAKE
Traidhfil nó cáca biotáille

This is a great Christmas favourite. Traditionally it should have home-made custard, but in this busy world packaged custard powder is used.

8 small sponge cakes
4 oz. raspberry jam
10 oz. medium sherry
2-3 tablsp. brandy
5 cups rich custard sauce
heavy cream
8 macaroons
12 ratafia biscuits (Almond cookies)
roasted almonds
grated rind of ½ lemon

Cut the sponge cakes in half, spread with the raspberry jam and put back together. Arrange them at the bottom of a large bowl. Cover with the ratafia biscuits and macaroons and then pour over the sherry and sprinkle the almonds and lemon rind. Prepare the custard as directed. Pour custard over the the mixture and leave to cool. Cover with whipped heavy cream and decorate with glace cherries, almonds and angelica.

Serves approximately 6

CUSTARD
Custaird

2 egg yolks
¼ cup sugar
1¼ cup milk
1½ tablsp. cornstarch
¼ cup milk
1 teasp. vanilla

IRISH WHISKEY CAKE
Ciste uisce beatha

This cake is best made the night before to get
the full flavour of the whiskey.

2/3 cup butter
2/3 cup sugar
2/3 cup flour
3 eggs
½ cup Irish whiskey
2/3 cup sultanas
1 teasp. baking soda
pinch of salt
peel of 1 lemon

Place the lemon peel in a glass covered with the
whiskey and leave overnight. Cream the butter
and sugar then sift the flour and add to mixture
together with the egg yolks, one at a time. Mix
well. Add the whiskey and the sultanas. Whisk
the egg whites stiffly and fold into the mixture
with the salt and baking soda. Place in a well-
greased 7 inch cake tin and bake in a preheated
350 oven for 1½ hours. Test before removing
from the oven.

If desired this cake can be decorated with
whipped cream to which has been added a few
drops of whiskey and glace cherries.

SHORTBREAD
Brioscaráí

Although Shortbread is traditionally Scottish
it has been in Ireland for several hundred
years. It is most popular at Christmas.

1½ cup flour
3 tablsp. sugar
3/4 cup butter
4 tablsp. milk
2 teasp. caraway (optional)

Mix the caraway seeds, if used, with the flour.
Melt the butter in the milk, then make a well
in the centre of the flour and pour in the
milk mixture and then the sugar. Mix well,
and knead lightly. Place on a floured board
and roll out to ¼in. thickness, into a circle,
or oblong. Place on a greased baking sheet
and if a circle, crimp the edges with your
finger and thumb.   If oblong, mark off in
squares. Prick all over with a fork. Cut
across the circle diagonally into 8 pieces.
Do not cut through the paste, but make a deep
incision. Place in a moderate oven, 350,
for 20 minutes, or until crisp and golden.
Cool on a wire rack, and dust with sugar.
Break the circle in the 8 pieces, or break
the oblong into squares, and serve.

Beat until creamy the egg yolks and sugar.
Scald the 1¼ cup milk and then pour over the
yolk mixture. Dissolve the cornstarch in
the ¼ cup milk and then stir this into the
yolk mixture. Stir and cook these ingredients over a very low heat until they are
thick. Cool them slightly then add the
vanilla.

URNEY PUDDING
Maróg Urnaidhe

*This is a very popular steamed pudding from
Northern Ireland.*

2 tablsp. strawberry jam (or your favourite)
1 tablsp. vanilla essence
1 teasp. baking soda
4 oz. butter
1 cup flour
2 tablsp. sugar
2 eggs, beaten

Cream the sugar and butter and then add
the beaten eggs and flour slowly. Add the
jam and vanilla and baking soda. Mix well
and place in a buttered basin, cover with
greaseproof and foil and tie with string.
Steam for 2 hours.

Serves 4

MEAD
Meá

Mead is an ancient Irish drink, probably being first made by the Monks. It is quite a sweet tasting wine and very potent after maturing.

17½ cups water
3 lb honey
2 oz fresh ginger
1 oz fresh yeast

Boil the water for half an hour then add the honey and allow to dissolve well. Boil for another hour. Grate the ginger and place in a muslin bag and add to the boiling liquid. Leave to cool until it does not burn your finger. Add the yeast. Pour into a large jar for fermentation, leaving an air space, and seal tightly. Keep at room temperature until the bubbling has stopped. Pour into bottles and cover lightly, but do not cork for 2 days, until fermentation has stopped. Cork tightly and store in dark cupboard for at least 6 months before drinking.

SCAILTÍN

*This is the Irish name for a hot whiskey drink
very popular when provincial Ireland
entertained lavishly. After a large meal,
a glass of port and scailtín must have given
the diners a sweet soporific feeling after
a busy day.*

1 teasp. honey
good measure of Irish whiskey
cup of hot milk
stick of cinammon

Blend the whiskey and honey together and then
stir in the hot milk and put the stick of
cinammon in the cup.

BISHOP'S NIGHTCAP
Scailtín fiona

1 bottle port wine
stick of cinammon
2 pieces fresh ginger
2 oranges
2 whole cloves
¼ teasp. mace
¼ teasp. allspice
6 lumps of sugar
zest of lemon

Place the cloves in the oranges and bake in
a moderate oven (350) for half an hour,
until soft. Place all the spices in a pan
with 1-1/3 cups water and bring to the boil.
Pour into a warmed bowl and add the sugar
which has been rubbed with zest of lemon.
Remove oranges from oven and cut into
quarters and place in bowl. Stir until the
sugar has dissolved. Heat the port, but do
not boil, then pour into the bowl and serve.

73

BLANCMANGE
Bánghlóthach

The blancmange, called a "shape" in Ireland has been popular for a couple of centuries. Sometimes the pudding, when cold, is studded with currants, and a face made with almonds and angelica, called "hedgehog."

5 cups milk
2 egg whites, stiffly beaten
3 tablsp. cornflour
½ cup sugar
pinch of salt
1 teasp. vanilla

Mix together the sugar, cornflour and salt with 3 tablsp. milk. Stir until smooth, then add to the warm milk and stir well. Return to heat and bring to a boil, stirring all the time. Remove from heat and stir until it cools, add the vanilla and egg whites, and stir until well blended. Pour into a wetted mould and leave to cool or place in refrigerator.

Serves approximately 4

74

SYLLABUB
Siolliabab

Syllabub is a very old dessert probably around the 16th Century , but its origin is unknown .

1-1/3 cups heavy cream
1/3 cup sherry
1/3 cup brandy
juice of 1 lemon
3 oz. confectioner's sugar

Beat the cream, but do not overbeat. Gradually whisk in the sugar, lemon juice and the sherry and brandy. The mixture should be very soft. Spoon into glasses or small dishes and chill. Serve with sponge fingers, cake or sweet biscuits.

Serves 4

BLACK CAP PUDDING
Maróg sútha dubha

½ cup blackcurrants, cleaned, topped and tailed
3 tablsp. sugar
2/3 cup fresh breadcrumbs
1/3 cup flour
½ tablsp butter
juice of 1 lemon
2 eggs, beaten
butter
1-1/3 cup milk

Butter a 5 cup pudding basin. Place the
blackcurrants in a pan with the lemon juice and
2 tablsp. sugar, cook slowly for 5 minutes.
Place in basin. Mix the flour, breadcrumbs
and remaining sugar in a bowl. Make a well in
the middle and add the beaten eggs and mix.
Add the milk and beat well. Let stand for
15 minutes. Pour over the blackcurrants,
cover with a cloth or foil and tie. Steam
for 2-2½ hours. Turn out so that the
blackcurrants "black cap" cover the pudding.

Serves approximately 4

IRISH MIST CREAM
Uachtar 'Irish Mist'

4 egg yolks
2 tablsp. honey
7 teasp. gelatine
2½ cups milk
1¼ cups whipping cream
¼ cup Irish Mist liqueur
4 egg whites, stiffly beaten

Bring the milk to a boil. In another bowl
mix the egg yolks and honey together. Keep
stirring and slowly add the boiling milk,
then return the mixture to the pan and stirring
constantly, cook until it thickens. Do not
boil. Dissolve the gelatine in small amount of
warm water and then add to the mixture. Stir
until the mixture cools. Add the Irish Mist,
3/4 of the whipped cream and fold in the egg
whites. Spoon the mixture into one large bowl
or several small moulds. Refrigerate until
set. Unmould and decorate with the remaining
whipped cream.

Serves approximately 4

CARRAGEEN CREAM or SYRUP
Sioróip carraigín

Carrageen Moss *is a type of seaweed brownish
black or dark green in colour which grows
on the rocks at low tide line. It is picked
in early summer during the spring tides and
bleached in the sun.   When it is quite white
it can be stored in a jute bag for up to 1 or 2
years.   The Irish feel it is very good for the
health because of the iodine content.*

1 oz. dried carrageen moss
2 oz. sugar
rind of ½ a lemon
2 teasp. whiskey or brandy (optional)
2¼ cups milk

Soak the dried Carrageen in cold water for about
20 minutes, drain and boil with the milk and
lemon rind for 15 minutes over a low heat,
stirring occasionally. until the milk thickens
slightly. Strain through a sieve, discard the
seaweed and return the milk to the pan with the
sugar, and whiskey or brandy if used. Heat
until the sugar is dissolved, and then pour into
a mould and leave to set in the refrigerator.
This cream can be used instead of custard.

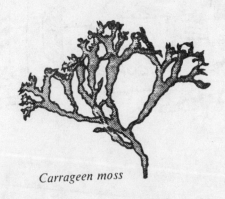

Carrageen moss

IRISH COFFEE
Caife Gaelach

Although Irish Coffee is not a traditional drink, because of its popularity it is fast becoming a 'tradition.'

Enough strong, black, hot coffee to fill the coffee cups within 2 inches of the top.
1 teasp. sugar for each cup
1 tablsp. heavy cream for each cup
generous measure of Irish Whiskey

Warm the Irish Coffee cups and then put in 1 teasp. sugar per cup. Add enough coffee to fill to within 2 inches of the top. Stir well to dissolve the sugar. Add the Irish Whiskey to fill within ½ inch of the top. Hold a teaspoon, curved side up, across the cup and pour 1 tablsp. heavy cream over each cup. Do not stir, and drink immediately.

HOT WATER PASTRY

4 cups plain flour
¼ lb. beef dripping or lard
1¼ cups water
½ teasp. salt

Place fat and water in a saucepan and bring to
the boil. Put the flour and salt in a basin
and make a hole in the middle, then pour the
boiling water and fat in and mix well until
cold enough to handle. Form into a ball.
Place on a floured board and knead well.
Divide pastry in half and keep one half warm.
Roll the other half out into a large oval,
then place a small jar in the middle. Mould
the pastry around the jar to about 3" in
height and about 3" across. Remove the jar
and make another mould in the same manner.
Roll out the lids, cutting them into rounds
to fit the top.

FLAKY PASTRY

2 cups flour
6 oz. lard and margarine mixed
cold water to mix
pinch of salt
few drops of lemon juice

Add the salt to the flour, and sieve them
into a mixing bowl. Soften the lard and
margarine, blending thoroughly. Divide
the softened fat into four equal portions.
Rub one portion of the fat into the sieved
flour and salt. Add a little lemon juice
and enough cold water to make an elastic
dough. Place the dough on a board and roll
it out into an oblong, keeping the sides

straight. Place one portion of the fat in
small pieces over two-thirds of the dough,
as shown below. Dredge the entire surface
with flour and fold bottom third up, and
the top third down. Turn pastry to bring
folded edge to right. Repeat rolling,
adding another portion of fat and folding
twice more. Repeat using remaining portion
of fat. Bake in a hot oven for about
15 minutes (450), then lower temperature
slightly and bake for a further 10-15
minutes.

SUET PASTRY

4 cups flour
1 cup suet, finely chopped
1¼ cups water
2 tablsp. baking soda
1½ teasp. salt

Mix all dry ingredients, then add cold water
to make an elastic consistency.   Use as
required. This pastry may be boiled, steamed
or baked.

OATMEAL PASTRY

½ cup flour
½ cup oatmeal
3-4 oz. margarine or cooking fat
cold water to mix
pinch of salt

Blend flour and oatmeal then rub in fat. Add
salt and mix to a very stiff consistency with
cold water. Work lightly until smooth. Roll
out and use as required.

POTATO PASTRY

½ cup flour
½ cup cooked potatoes (sieved)
2 teasp. baking soda
½ teasp. salt
2½ oz. margarine

Rub margarine into sieved flour and baking
powder. Mix in sieved potatoes and add water
to make a stiff dough. Roll out and use as
shortcrust pastry.

SHORT CRUST PASTRY

This pastry can be made with cooking fat, butter, margarine or a mixture of these fats. These cooking fats give a very crisp crumbly pastry.

2 cups plain flour
1/2 cup fat
pinch of sugar and salt
cold water to mix

Sieve the flour, salt and sugar. Cut the fat into small pieces and place in a bowl. Rub the mixture together with your fingers until it is like breadcrumbs. Gradually add water to the mixture to bind ingredients together. Form the pastry into a ball and place on lightly floured pastry board. Roll out into an oblong about 1/4 inch thick. Roll in one direction and lift the pastry and turn it. This is to stretch the pastry evenly. Short crust pastry is cooked in an oven 425-450.

To make sweet short crust pastry add 1/8 cup of sugar to the flour and salt.

This pastry can be prepared in advance. It should be stored uncooked in foil in the re-frigerator or freezer. It may also be baked as a pastry shell and then stored in an air-tight tin.

ROUGH PUFF PASTRY

Proportions for 9 inch pie crust

2 cups bread flour
1/2 teasp. salt
6 tablsp. unsalted butter
6 tablsp. lard
1 egg diluted with 1 tablsp. water
6 tablsp. ice water
1/2 teasp. lemon juice

Sift flour, then resift with salt. Cut
butter and lard into pieces about 1 inch in
size, then mix lightly with flour. Make a
well in the centre. Add a little water. Mix
lightly, keeping butter and lard intact. Add
remaining ice water and lemon juice to form
moderately stiff dough. Roll dough into an
oblong. Fold equally in three. Turn pastry
so that you have a folded edge to the right
and left. Roll it again. Repeat another
four times. Let stand in cool place 1/2 hour
to 1 hour. Brush pastry with egg mixture
when it is half cooked to give it a glaze.
This dough may be used for all types of rolls,
pies and vol au vent cases, etc.

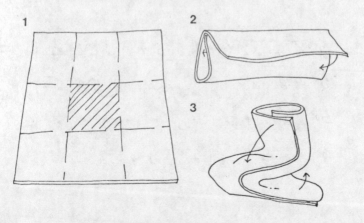

The Soldier's Song

We'll sing a song, a soldier's song
With cheering, rousing chorus,
As round our blazing fires we throng,
The starry heavens o'er us;
Impatient for the coming fight,
And as we 'wait the morning's light,
Here in the silence of the night,
We'll chant a soldier's song.

Soldiers are we, whose lives are pledged
   to Ireland;
Some have come from a land beyond
   the wave,
Sworn to be free, no more our ancient
   sireland
Shall shelter the despot or the slave,
Tonight we man the 'bearna baoil'*
In Erin's cause, come woe or weal;
'Mid cannons' roar and rifles peal
We'll chant a soldier's song.

(*gap of danger)

Amhrán na bhFiann

Seo dhibh, a chairde, duan ógláigh,
Cathréimeach, bríomhar, ceolmhar,
Ár dtinte cnámh go buacach táid,
'S an spéir go min réaltógach,
Is fonnmhar faobhrach sinn chun gleo,
'S go tiúnmhar glé roimh thíocht don ló,
Faoi chiúnas caomh na hoiche ar seol,
Seo libh, canaíg amhrán na bhFiann.

Sinne Fianna Fáil, atá faoi gheall
    ag Éirinn,
Buíon dár slua thar toinn do ráinig
    chugainn,
Faoi mhóid bheith saor, Seantír ár
    sinsear feasta
Ni fhágfar faoin tiorán ná faoin tráill.
Anocht a théam sa bhearna baoil,
Le gean ar Ghaeil chun báis nó saoil,
Le gunna-scréach, faoi lámhach na bpiléar,
Seo libh, canaíg amhrán na bhFiann.